SPOTLIGHT ON THE AMERICAN INDIANS OF CALIFORNIA

THE
TONGVA

MARY GRAHAM

NEW YORK

Published in 2018 by The Rosen Publishing Group, Inc.
29 East 21st Street, New York, NY 10010

Editor: Melissa Raé Shofner
Book Design: Michael Flynn
Interior Layout: Rachel Rising

Photo Credits: Cover Marilyn Angel Wynn/Corbis Documentary/Getty Images; p. 5 Michele and Tom Grimm/Alamy Stock Photo; p. 7 Kayte Deioma/Alamy Stock Photo; p. 9 Nature and Science/Alamy Stock Photo; pp. 10, 11 Courtesy of the Autry's Collection; p. 12 Menno Schaefer/Shutterstock.com; p. 13 Phillip Rubino/Shutterstock.com; p. 15 Don Graham/FlixrImages; p. 17 Carlos Chavez/Contributor/Los Angeles Times/Getty Images; p. 19 Andrew Zarivny/Shutterstock.com; p. 21 Bruce Yuanyue Bi/Lonely Planet Images/Getty Images; p. 23 https://commons.wikimedia.org/wiki/File:The_E.O.C._Ord%27s_first_map_of_the_city_of_Los_Angeles,_drawn_in_August_29,_1849_(CHS-6040).jpg; p. 25 Nagel Photography/Shutterstock.com; p. 27 https://commons.wikimedia.org/wiki/File:Carleton_Watkins_(American_-_(Mission,_San_Fernando_Rey)_-_Google_Art_Project.jpg; p. 29 https://commons.wikimedia.org/wiki/File:Statue_of_Juana_Maria_and_child.jpg.

Cataloging-in-Publication Data

Names: Graham, Mary.
Title: The Tongva / Mary Graham.
Description: New York : PowerKids Press, 2018. | Series: Spotlight on the American Indians of California | Includes index.
Identifiers: ISBN 9781508162872 (pbk.) | ISBN 9781538324974 (library bound) | ISBN 9781508162926 (6 pack)
Subjects: LCSH: Gabrielino Indians--Juvenile literature. | Indians of North America--California--Juvenile literature.
Classification: LCC E99.G15 G73 2018 | DDC 979.4'00497--dc23

Manufactured in China

CONTENTS

CHAPTER ONE

THE EARLY TONGVA PEOPLE

The Tongva people once lived in an area of California that included much of what is now Los Angeles County and northern Orange County. The **ancestors** of the Tongva lived along the coast and became excellent fishermen. They traveled farther away from the shoreline in their canoes and eventually built new communities on distant coastal islands. By AD 500, the Tongva region included nearly all the communities that were present when the first Spanish explorers reached California.

The Tongva people's way of life would undergo few changes over the next 1,200 years. However, in 1771, the Tongva's lives were changed forever by the arrival of Europeans. Their experience with the Europeans was filled with conflict. As the decades passed, the Tongva population grew smaller. By 1900, some scholars believed there were no Tongva people left.

Today, some of the surviving members of the Tongva group are working to rebuild their community. By preserving their **heritage**, they hope to share the story of their ancestors with other people.

CHAPTER TWO

SETTLEMENTS AND HOMES

The Tongva people likely lived in large towns and small villages. Some towns may have had up to 50 homes and more than 200 people. Small villages may have had 12 or fewer people.

Most of the Tongva lived in small, rounded houses made from wooden poles, brush, and reeds. These single-family homes were often about 10 feet (3 m) across. The middle of each house had a fire pit that was used for heat and cooking. A hole in the center of the roof allowed light to enter and smoke to escape. Family members slept on reed mats.

The Tongva people who settled in larger towns on the coastal islands lived in similar kinds of houses. However, these structures were much bigger, and each housed up to four related families. They were often built with whale ribs instead of wooden poles.

In coastal settlements, the doorways of most homes faced the sea. This helped keep out the cold winds that sometimes blew down the slopes of nearby mountains.

CHAPTER THREE

PREPARING MEALS

The early Tongva people ate many kinds of wild plants and animals. The Pacific Ocean provided the Tongva people with much of their food. They ate many kinds of fish and shellfish, as well as seaweed and larger sea animals, such as seals and dolphins.

The women often prepared meals and created dishes using many different methods. The women had to grind or smash some foods—such as abalone, a type of sea snail—to make them soft enough to eat. Most fruits and berries didn't require any preparation.

Most food was cooked outside over an open flame. Tongva women also knew how to steam and smoke their meals. Slabs of stone were used as frying pans. Hot rocks were placed inside cooking baskets to heat soups and stews. Some foods could be salted, dried, or smoked. This preserved the food so it could be traded or stored for later use.

This painting shows the Tongva people preparing their food. Some of the plants they ate, such as acorns, had to be ground into powder and washed several times in water to remove poisons.

CHAPTER FOUR

CRAFTING USEFUL TOOLS

The Tongva people produced many beautiful and useful items using the natural resources around them. They chipped stones to form weapons and tools, such as arrowheads, spearpoints, and knives. They also made stone tools for grinding nuts and seeds. Cooking pots, jars, and smoking pipes were made from clay.

Women combined different kinds of plants to weave baskets, which they decorated with beautiful patterns. They made bowls, dishes, jars, and other useful items. Some baskets were woven so tightly they could hold water.

Men made items such as bowls, cups, jars, musical instruments, and spoons from wood. They made plants into strong strings and ropes. The Tongva also used plant fibers to make nets, bags, belts, and many other similar objects.

The Tongva made many items from the animals they hunted. Women used furs and skins to make clothing and blankets. Hunters and warriors used rattlesnake poison to make their arrowheads deadlier. Tongva craftspeople also made clothing, jewelry, tools, musical instruments, and other objects from bones, feathers, and seashells.

CHAPTER FIVE

TONGVA SOCIETY

The family was the smallest Tongva social group. Together, several families formed a clan. The largest social group was the village. The oldest male member of a group was usually its leader. In the villages, the political leaders were called *tumia'r*, or chiefs.

Tongva society was also divided into groups based

Members of a clan were believed to share a common animal ancestor, such as a bear, an eagle, or a coyote. Tongva clans formed two larger groups, called moieties. Moieties helped to regulate trade and other kinds of relations.

BLACK BEAR

BALD EAGLE

on money and respect. The chiefs, their families, and rich men formed the highest rank of this society. Some of the older families and people of above-average wealth formed a middle group. Almost everyone else was considered to be a commoner. Those of the lowest social rank included war prisoners and slaves.

The Tongva people had religious leaders who also served as doctors. Most of them were men. These religious healers were believed to have special powers that could be used for good or evil. Because of this, they were widely respected and sometimes feared.

CHAPTER SIX

LEADING THE TONGVA PEOPLE

The basic unit of the Tongva people's government was the village or town. The *tumia'r* ruled the community. He was responsible for settling arguments, making decisions, leading his people in war, and planning most religious ceremonies.

A person became a *tumia'r* because their father was a *tumia'r*. A woman was sometimes allowed to become a political or religious leader if a family didn't have a son. Village leaders sometimes formed temporary **alliances**, which allowed a single chief to rule combined communities.

The Tongva people went to war for many reasons. Sometimes they fought to defend themselves against outsiders. They also fought other Tongva villages over territory or for revenge. Every village had its own territory. Anyone who tried to hunt or gather food in these areas without **permission** could be attacked.

The Tongva people gathered for ceremonies in structures such as the one seen here. The *tumia'r* was often in charge of planning these ceremonies.

CHAPTER SEVEN

RELIGIOUS RITUALS

Religion was very important to the Tongva people. Most of their holidays involved their faith. They had religious **rituals** to trace the path of a person from birth to death, and funeral services were particularly important. Other celebrations marked the passing seasons. Many of the Tongva religious services emphasized the need to balance the powers that existed in the universe. Sickness, death, and destruction could result if these powers fell out of balance.

Tongva religious rituals usually involved songs and dances. The men often performed sacred dances while the women sang. Religious leaders wore special clothing and paint that made them look like animals or supernatural beings.

The Tongva people created rock art. Sometimes they used paint to mark rocks with pictures called pictographs. Sometimes they scratched symbols into the outer surface of rocks to make petroglyphs. The Tongva also made special kinds of sand paintings by creating designs with colored sand.

Robert Dorame, shown here, is a **descendant** of the Tongva people. He burns sage as a sign of respect for his ancestors.

CHAPTER EIGHT

EARLY SPANISH CONTACT

Juan Rodríguez Cabrillo, a Spanish explorer, was the first European to meet the Tongva people. In 1542, while exploring the California coast, Cabrillo discovered the Tongva living on San Pedro and Santa Catalina Islands. He found them to be friendly and interested in trading.

During the 200 years that followed, other Spanish ships visited California. The Tongva people probably met with many of the ships' crews and might have even traded with them. It's very likely that European diseases, such as smallpox and measles, killed many of the Tongva people, just as they killed large numbers of American Indians in other parts of California and North America.

In 1769, Spain launched an expedition to occupy California. By this time, many of the Tongva people had likely died from European diseases. They may have been working to slowly regrow their population.

Juan Rodríguez Cabrillo was the first European to explore the West Coast of North America. Cabrillo National Monument, shown here, was created in 1913. It looks out over San Diego Bay, which Cabrillo discovered in 1542.

CHAPTER NINE

SPANISH MISSIONS

In the mid-1700s, Carlos III, king of Spain, began to worry that another country might occupy California. In 1769, he sent an expedition to bring the region under Spanish control.

In 1771, the Spanish established Mission San Gabriel in California. Missions were centers of religious instruction and communities in which Europeans taught their ways of life. They were also outposts where Spanish officials worked with American Indians toward common goals.

The **missionaries** needed to get the American Indians to live and work at the missions. Some Tongva people were drawn in by the steel weapons, new animals, and new foods the Spanish brought with them. Others were unsure about these gifts. Most of the people at the missions thought they would be able to keep their traditional ways of life. However, it was soon obvious that there was no place in the missions for the Tongva faith.

Some of the Tongva decided that they wanted to live in the missions and become neophytes, or new followers. Individuals, as well as whole villages of Tongva people, moved to Mission San Gabriel.

CHAPTER TEN

MISSION SAN GABRIEL

Mission San Gabriel's history is troubled. There were many difficult days during its first 10 years. During this time, the Tongva warriors and the Spanish soldiers who were assigned to protect the mission fought a number of battles against each other. In one of these conflicts, the soldiers started trouble with the American Indians, cruelly attacking one of the Tongva women. The mission priests and the American Indians demanded that the governor of California punish the troops.

San Gabriel was soon hit by another disaster. Floods washed away the first mission buildings, and a new settlement had to be created some distance away. Despite these setbacks, more and more Tongva people moved to the mission. By 1778, most of the people in nearby villages had moved to Mission San Gabriel. Some Tongva people, however, still didn't want to live at the mission.

Los Angeles was established in 1781. In the late 1700s, Tongva people who didn't want to live at the missions sometimes worked for Spanish settlers who lived in Los Angeles. This survey map of the area was made in 1849.

PLAN
De la ciudad
DE LOS
ANGELES

Surveyed & Drawn by

E.O.C. Ord Lt. U.S.A. &
Wm. R. Hutton Asst.
August 29th 1849

23

CHAPTER ELEVEN

TROUBLE AT THE MISSIONS

By 1800, it was almost impossible for the Tongva people to live in a traditional way. The remaining Tongva realized the new settlers couldn't be ignored. Some finally gave up and moved into the missions.

A small number of Tongva led secret lives in the mountains and canyons. Other Tongva joined with American Indian tribes that lived to the northeast, in California's immense central valley. Occasionally, they returned to **raid** the Spanish settlements. The number and strength of the attacks against the missions gradually grew. After 1810, the neighboring Mohave people also began to attack the Tongva and their Spanish **allies**.

Despite the troubles, the Tongva people continued to move to the missions. The missions had more than enough food and trade goods to support the Tongva who lived there. The missions grew and appeared successful, but they still had many serious problems.

The Spanish established Mission San Fernando in 1797 in hopes of **recruiting** the remaining northern Tongva. Many of these Tongva people had already adopted European ways of life, such as farming and living in Spanish-style buildings.

CHAPTER TWELVE

MEXICO AND THE MISSIONS

In 1822, Spain abandoned its claim to California and Mexico took over. The Tongva people living in the area were now citizens of Mexico. Mexican officials wanted to end the missions and promised the Tongva neophytes complete control of their towns and all other mission property.

However, the promises of a better future grew dim as a series of delays prevented the Mexican government from completing its plan to end the missions. The attacks from the Mohave continued. The neophytes and the Spaniards also had to fight off new raids by Yokuts warriors from the north.

The Mexican government's promises were never fulfilled. Instead, Mexican settlers from Los Angeles took almost everything from the Tongva people who lived at the missions. Nearly everything they'd worked so hard to create and defend was gone.

Between 1833 and 1835, the populations of Mission San Gabriel and Mission San Fernando, shown here, **declined** as Mexican officials moved to end the missions.

CHAPTER THIRTEEN

LIFE AFTER THE MISSIONS

The end of the missions hit the Tongva people hard. Most Tongva people may have taken up jobs working for wealthy Mexican ranchers or townspeople. Enemy American Indian groups from the north and the east, along with Mexicans, attacked any remaining Tongva populations.

After the United States took over California in 1848, a small group of Tongva individuals living in the traditional way continued to cling to survival in what had once been eastern Tongva territory.

In 1850, when California became a U.S. state, the new government did nothing to improve the situation for the Tongva people. Diseases, **discrimination**, and poverty brought an early end to the lives of many of the mission survivors. By 1900, very few people, including the Tongva, identified themselves as descendants of the mission American Indians. It seemed as though the Tongva people had vanished.

Juana Maria was believed to be the last remaining member of the Nicoleño people, a Tongva group that lived on San Nicolas Island off the coast of California. Juana Maria's story inspired Scott O'Dell's 1960 novel *Island of the Blue Dolphins*.

CHAPTER FOURTEEN

PRESERVING THEIR HERITAGE

Today, no one is sure exactly how many Tongva people remain, but scholars have estimated their population to be somewhere between a few hundred to a few thousand. It's hard to get an exact count because, unlike many of the other California American Indians, the Tongva don't have a **reservation**.

Individuals from the Tongva community are fighting to save the parts of their traditional lands that haven't been turned into modern cities. Tongva people have also fought against government organizations to save their sacred places and restore Tongva religious traditions. Their **artifacts** and artwork can be seen in a number of important museums in the United States and Europe. However, much of the natural world that the ancient Tongva lived in is gone. The Tongva people are working hard to preserve their surviving traditions while their long struggle for justice continues.

GLOSSARY

alliance (uh-LY-unts) A close association formed between people or groups of people to reach a common objective.

ally (AA-ly) One of two or more people or groups who work together.

ancestor (AN-ses-tuhr) Someone in your family who lived long before you.

artifact (AR-tih-fakt) Something made by humans in the past that still exists.

decline (dih-KLYN) To become less in amount.

descendant (dih-SEN-dent) Someone related to a person or group of people who lived at an earlier time.

discrimination (dis-krih-muh-NAY-shun) Treating people unequally based on class, race, or religion.

heritage (HEHR-uh-tihj) The traditions and beliefs that are part of the history of a group or nation.

missionary (MIH-shuh-nehr-ee) Someone who travels to a new place to spread their faith.

permission (puhr-MIH-shun) The approval of a person in charge.

raid (RAYD) A surprise attack by an enemy.

recruit (ree-KROOT) To convince people to join a group.

reservation (reh-zuhr-VAY-shun) Land set aside by the government for specific American Indian nations to live on.

ritual (RIH-choo-uhl) A religious ceremony, especially one consisting of a series of actions performed in a certain order.

INDEX

PRIMARY SOURCE LIST

Page 11
Gabrieliño basket tray. San Gabriel, CA. ca. early 1900s. From the Caroline Boeing Poole Collection. Now held at the Autry Museum of the American West, Los Angeles, CA.

Page 23
E. O. C. Ord's first map of the city of Los Angeles. Edward O. C. Ord and William Hutton. Photograph by Charles C. Pierce. August 29, 1849. Now held by the University of Southern California, USC Libraries Special Collections.

Page 27
Mission San Fernando Rey. Photograph. Carleton Watkins. ca. 1880. Now held at the Getty Center, Los Angeles, CA.

WEBSITES

Due to the changing nature of Internet links, PowerKids Press has developed an online list of websites related to the subject of this book. This site is updated regularly. Please use this link to access the list: www.powerkidslinks.com/saic/ton